B. R. C.

A Trip to the Rockies

.

B. R. C.

A Trip to the Rockies

ISBN/EAN: 9783337138844

Printed in Europe, USA, Canada, Australia, Japan

Cover: Foto ©Andreas Hilbeck / pixelio.de

More available books at **www.hansebooks.com**

A TRIP TO THE ROCKIES

BY

B. R. C.

———

NEW YORK
The Knickerbocker Press
1890

The Knickerbocker Press, New York
Electrotyped and Printed by
G. P. Putnam's Sons

TO THE "DALMATIA" PARTY

THE MOST INTELLIGENT AND CONGENIAL COMPANY

OF TOURISTS THAT THE

" SKY-KISSING CLIFFS AND PRAIRIES PRANKED WITH FLOWERS "

EVER WELCOMED

WHOSE ASSOCIATION WILL EVER BE CHERISHED AMONG THE

" PLEASURES OF MEMORY "

THIS BOOK IS RESPECTFULLY INSCRIBED

Journeys are memoried in light or shade ;
This one in sunlight, when, by chance,
Strangers to most, all ages and all whims,
We for a fortnight sojourned far from home ;
A memory, where the heart and eye
Replete, lie still and dream again.
God gave the view—a human heart the feast.
What star of fortune brought our lives
In happy contact ?   Here we trace
The secret of our rare content—
The outline of each happy day.

E. H. S.

A Trip to the Rockies.

FOR three months—since my first visit to Kansas in June last—the anticipation of another visit had been uppermost in many minds.

The writer was authorized by Mr. Blanchard to select a party of bankers and business men of New York and Brooklyn to attend the annual convention of the " American Bankers' Association," to be held in Kansas City, September 24th and 25th. To add to the growing interest, already manifested in the trip by the elect, a telegram was received, as follows : " Hutchinson, Kansas, July 23d. Each guest will have a section, and is cordially invited to bring his wife.—Ben Blanchard." This telegram was the keystone to the arch. Had the Pullman Company been able to furnish a larger car, our number would have been doubled. As the car was too long to go over the B. & O., via Washington, Harper's Ferry, and Cumberland Gap, on account of the short curves, we went via Pennsylvania through Harrisburg, Johnstown, and Altoona.

The ever-watchful reporter was on hand, and the following description from the Brooklyn *Standard-Union* was a very good report of our car and company as we left Jersey City, September 23d.

"A large party of Brooklynites crossed Fulton Ferry early this morning, most of the men carrying gripsacks and the ladies satchels. It was evidently a party of tourists ; and the wide-awake wage-workers, who were crossing the ferry at the same time, recognizing some of the best-known people of the ' City of Churches ' in the party, wondered what was going on. They dismissed the subject from their minds eventually, arriving at the conclusion that they were a small party off on a little pleasure trip. In one respect they were right. The party was off on a pleasure trip, but it was not a little one. In fact it was a very large one, and the *Standard-Union* reporter learned all the particulars. He ascertained that the American Bankers' Association hold their annual convention at Kansas City on Wednesday and Thursday next, and the party who started from Brooklyn were bound for there. Among the party were Ben Blanchard, President of the Empire Loan and Trust Company, of Hutchinson, Kan.; Hon. Darwin R. James and Mrs. James ; Hon. John Jay Knox, President Bank of the Republic, late Comptroller U. S. Currency, accompanied by his two daughters, Miss Carrie and Miss Bessie Knox ; Edward

Merritt, President Long Island Loan and Trust Company, and Mrs. Merritt; Hon. D. O. Bradley, President Tarrytown National Bank, and Mrs. Bradley; Capt. Ambrose Snow, President New York Board of Trade; Frank W. Shaw, M.D.; Crowell Hadden, President Long Island Bank, and Mrs. Hadden; Miss Louise I. Shannon, Miss Jeanie S. Corwin, Miss Jennie S. Brush; Major B. R. Corwin, Eastern Manager Empire Loan and Trust Co., and Mrs. Corwin, and others.

"They went in Mr. Blanchard's special car, the Dalmatia, which was attached to the fast express of the Pennsylvania Railroad. The elegant car was most magnificently decorated with silk flags and flowers, and every possible provision was made for not only the comfort but royal entertainment of the tourists. An excellent library, beautiful portfolios, dainty note-books bound in Russian leather, checkers, chess, dominos, and other games, and in fact every thing that could possibly be thought of to fan the leaden wings of time, were placed at the disposal of the party. One of the sets of dominos that were in the car was made of genuine shell pearl, and is the costliest set in the country. They are the property of Mr. Blanchard, and have accompanied him on thousands of miles of journeys. The flag decoration of the car was done by Fred Aldridge, of this city, and the floral decorations by Florist Weir, of Clinton Street. The party left

Jersey City at 9 o'clock this morning, expecting to arrive at St. Louis Tuesday evening, and Kansas City Wednesday morning."

As our party entered the " Dalmatia " there were expressions of delight from all. It was a perfect bower of roses. We laid aside our wraps, had a moment to say good-bye to friends and then our train rolled out of the depot and rushed on westward bound.

We were very much disappointed that E. H. Pullen,· Esq., Cashier of the Bank of the Republic, and Mrs. Pullen could not go with us,—we could not have both the president and chief executive officer. We would have included Asst. Cashier Stout if possible. James P. Stearns, Esq., Cashier of the Shawmut National Bank of Boston, and Mrs. Stearns, and John A. Nexsen, Esq., Cashier of the Fulton Bank of Brooklyn, and Mrs. Nexsen, General C. T. Christensen and Mrs. Christensen, Wm. H. Hazzard, Esq., President of the Fulton Bank of Brooklyn, and Mrs. Hazzard, and Mark W. Stevens, Esq., President of the Schoharie County Bank, and Mrs. Stevens, were among the invited guests, and were detained by circumstances that could not be controlled.

The day was beautiful. Our party were charmed with their surroundings. The morning hours vanished all too soon, and lunch was announced. It was our first introduction to the cuisine of the " Dalmatia," and one that will not soon be forgotten. Speeding along at sixty miles an hour, seated in a luxuriantly appointed vestibuled Pullman palace car, surrounded by a party of congenial friends, enjoying a lunch second to none, is an experience peculiarly well fitted to make one in good humor with himself and all the world.

At Philadelphia the railroad officials met us at the depot to see if any thing had been forgotten that would add to our comfort.

The afternoon flew away from us fully as fast as we were flying from New York. Dinner was called. Such a dinner ! We spent over two hours enjoying it, and only stopped to take a view of the ruins of Johnstown. It was dark, but the electric lights and the many torches of the workmen gave us a weird view of the desolation never to be forgotten. We crossed the Stone Bridge of dreadful memories safely, and soon after retired to our comfortable sleeping apartments, and slept soundly while we continued our journey at undiminished speed.

At Indianapolis we were met by the General Passenger Agent of the Bee Line, who extended to us every courtesy. After holding the train nearly an hour for us, that we might get a glimpse of Indiana's capital, he gave us a rapid run to Terre Haute at a mile a minute gait. After a beautiful day we ran into a heavy shower just as the lights of St. Louis came into

view across the Father of Waters.   After crossing the
wonderful structure over the Mississippi, second only
to the Brooklyn bridge, we rolled into the St. Louis
Union Depot exactly on time.   " What crowds of people ! '' was the exclamation from each of our party.   The
General Agent of the Missouri Pacific Railroad came
with us from Indianapolis and had our car attached at
once to the fast express on this favorite line to Kansas
City.   After a second night's refreshing sleep, morning found us steaming into the city five minutes ahead
of time.

We were to attend the convention of the American
Bankers' Association.   At the depot we were met by
the committee, ex-Governor Crittenden, and leading
bankers.   The convention was large, and its discus-
sions were interesting.

The most important topic for consideration before
the Association was the proposition to substitute Silver
Certificates for "Legal-Tender and National Bank
Notes.''   The speech of ex-Comptroller John Jay
Knox, who was one of our party, was unanswerable,
and should be recorded as an incident of our
journey.   We say, like the boy blowing the organ
to the professor at the key-board : "We did that
nicely, sir.''

"The proposition of Mr. St. John involves the with-
drawal of the legal-tender notes, the disbursement of

the $100,000,000 of gold, pledged as security for the redemption of these notes, the increased issue of silver coinage and of silver certificates from $2,000,000 worth to $4,000,000 per month, and finally the giving of these silver certificates the quality of legal tender.

" Mr. St. John, we all know, is sincere, is honest in the advocacy of his opinions ; but to me it is as clear as the light of day, that every one of these propositions is unwise and impracticable, if not grievously, flagrantly wrong.   Do the gentlemen of the convention know that the proposition giving the legal-tender quality to circulating notes was discussed by the people of this country previous to the adoption of the Constitution ; and that it was, perhaps, the most difficult question that was considered by the Fathers in the convention that prepared and finally adopted the Constitution of the United States.

" The question involves such serious, such far-reaching consequences that its discussion has been avoided by all the great financiers, by all the public men of this country from the outset.   From time to time it has been brought before Congress and laid aside as impracticable and unwise,* but finally placed upon the statute-book, not as a measure of choice, not because

* " United States Notes.   A History of the Various Issues of the Paper Money of the United States."   Chas. Scribner's Sons, New York, third edition, 1888, pp. 16, 33, 43, 117, 216.

any considerable number of members of Congress believed in it, but because they reluctantly came to the conclusion that it was a measure necessary to provide for carrying on a civil war unequalled in the history of nations.

" Does this convention propose to decide in an hour or a day, a new question of legal tender when it is known that the original proposition has been under consideration ever since the organization of this government, and finally passed only as a means of salvation in the midst of a great war? Does this convention in a moment propose to consider and decide a new question of legal tender, when it is known that the original question was before the Supreme Court of the United States for consideration for weeks and months? The Supreme Court of the United States, presumed to be composed of the greatest men in this country and of the greatest jurists of these times, have twice reversed their own judgment on this subject. First, they decided that the legal-tender act was unconstitutional ; secondly, they decided that the constitutionality of the legal-tender notes was based upon the war powers of Congress ; and their third decision—to the surprise of the country—was that Congress has power to issue legal-tender circulating notes to an unlimited extent in time of peace as well as in time of war.

"The legal-tender note which we have is a promise to pay. It is a promise to pay one hundred cents in gold, and every man in and out of Congress knows that it is a promise to pay one hundred cents in gold, and also that we have held almost from the date of the issue of the legal-tender note to the present time $100,000,000 of gold in the Treasury with which to pay or redeem these notes. This $100,000,000 of gold was first set aside for that purpose by a Republican Administration, but subsequently by a Democratic Administration, so that both of the great parties of the country are thoroughly committed to it. First, a Republican Administration has set aside this $100,000,000 in the Treasury sacred for the purpose of redeeming every dollar of legal-tender paper money which may be presented for payment. Secondly, the Secretary of the Treasury, Daniel Manning, and Conrad N. Jordan, the Treasurer of the United States, devised a new system of debt statement. The Treasury statement prepared by John Sherman was not satisfactory to the Democratic Administration of President Cleveland. For that reason his Secretary of the Treasury and his Treasurer of the United States devised a new statement, and took this $100,000,000 out of the general fund in which it was placed by their predecessors, thus proclaiming to all the world that it was not to be even thought of as available for general expenditures thereafter, but was to be left there as a sacred fund in gold to be paid to every man in this country upon the presentation of these legal-tender notes.

"And what now does the gentleman propose to substitute for these legal-tender notes which are secured *

* March 18, 1869. An Act was passed in which the United States "solemnly pledges its faith to make provision at the earliest possible period for the redemption of United States notes in coin."

Quotation from Act of Congress, approved January 14, 1875 :

"And on and after the first day of January, Anno Domini eighteen hundred and seventy-nine, the Secretary of the Treasury shall redeem, in coin of the United States legal-tender notes, then outstanding, on their presentation for redemption at the office of the Assistant Treasurer of the United States in the City of New York, in sums of not less than fifty dollars. And to enable the Secretary of the Treasury to prepare and provide for the redemption in this Act authorized or required, he is authorized to use any surplus revenues, from time to time, in the Treasury not otherwise appropriated, and to issue, sell, and dispose of, at not less than par, in coin, either of the description of bonds of the United States described in the Act of Congress approved July fourteenth, eighteen hundred and seventy, entitled ' An Act to Authorize the Re-Funding of the National Debt,' with like qualities, privileges, and exemptions to the extent necessary to carry this Act into full effect, and to use the proceeds thereof for the purpose aforesaid."

An Act to provide for the resumption of specie payments, approved January, 14, 1875.

Extract from Section 12, Act of July 12, 1882 :

"That the Secretary of the Treasury shall suspend the issue of such gold certificates whenever the amount of gold coin and gold bullion in the Treasury reserved for the redemption of the United States notes falls below $100,000,000."

Act approved July 12, 1882.

not only by $100,000,000 of gold, but by your property and my property, and by the property of every citizen, by the resources of the whole country. What does he propose to substitute for this promise to pay? This promise made by this great nation, which it is bound to keep or be disgraced, as you or I would be disgraced if we should not meet our obligations? He proposes to substitute warehouse receipts—these are his words, not mine—warehouse receipts, which he himself acknowledges to-day to have an intrinsic value of but $71\frac{1}{2}$ cents.

" He proposes a new doctrine, never before heard of either in or out of Congress, to make, not a promise to pay (of the nation) a legal tender, but what he calls a silver warehouse receipt, a legal tender, which you and I shall be forced to take in full payment no matter what may be its value.

" This is a new doctrine, gentlemen; it is a doctrine that we should go slow about; that should be well considered by the best financial minds of this country. I venture to say that if it goes before Congress it will not be decided in one session; it will not get out of the hands of committee in one session; it involves the financial history of this country from the time of Thomas Jefferson down to the present date. Gentlemen who suppose that they can, upon hearing one paper read with a few figures, come to an intelligent conclusion upon

the subject, deceive themselves. Such a subject should
be considered seriously in all its bearings, and if so considered, mark my words, it will be declined.

" Furthermore, what else does this proposition seek
to do?

" The proposition is that we shall issue certificates
which the gentleman calls warehouse receipts, based
upon a silver dollar now worth 71½ cents, and then
keep on buying silver bullion until it advances 28
cents on the dollar, making the dollar worth intrinsi-
cally 99½ cents.

" Was any merchant in the history of the world ever
known to go into the market and buy wheat or corn or
oats, or any marketable property, and to continue to buy
it day in and day out, week in and week out, month in
and month out, year in and year out, upon a rising
market created by himself ! We have all heard of
corners in stock in New York, and corners in wheat in
Chicago, where speculators not infrequently raise the
price of stocks or of wheat to a high and false value by
a trick, and then oblige other people to buy their accu-
mulation at fictitious value in order to fulfil their con-
tracts ! But no man ever before heard of an individual
or a nation making a corner upon himself or itself and
obliging himself or the nation to buy other people's com-
modities at high and false values created by the pur-
chaser ! Gentlemen, do you propose to do this foolish
thing ? I hope not. This Convention of Bankers has

from the beginning shown itself to be a conservative body on all these questions. I beg you to remain conservative. Let the Congress of the United States consider these subjects and take the responsibility. I know of no question that has ever been introduced here and sent to Congress for consideration of which I would be ashamed. But it is not for us to say that we can comprehend in an hour these great questions of legal tender which the Supreme Court has taken years to consider. And I hope their last decision will not long hence be again reversed by a new court that may arise. I believe with George Bancroft,* that some day or other it will be reversed, and that it will be held that legal tender is a thing to be issued in time of war only. Kings and crowns have clipped the dollar ; they have cut it down one half and two thirds and three fourths. Nobody but tyrants can force a poor man to take 70 cents for 100 cents in gold, or 30 cents, or any sum less than 100 cents exactly. Gentlemen, I entreat you to go slow on this subject. Nothing is lost by a little time. You might not decide in a day a transaction involving but $10,000 in your own banks. You would not decide in an hour unless you knew every thing about the subject. Let us consider these four great propositions wisely and diligently, and then be able to give an intelligent reason for our decision.''

* A Plea for the Constitution. George Bancroft. Harper & Brothers. 1886.

Mr. Knox was frequently applauded. Then Mr. Sneed again came forward. "Gentlemen," he remarked, "I had not intended to say any thing more on this subject; I am not going to make a speech. But my friend Mr. Knox, known to all as a man of the very highest character—and I say that there is no man among those who compose this body for whom I have a higher regard; I have served with him in these conventions since their organization; I know him not only to be fair and generous and just, but he is more, he is a man—and I say it without disparagement to any other man in this convention—who has given this subject and other subjects of finance his most careful consideration. But we are all inclined to run in a groove; it is natural. And I believe that Mr. Knox is just as honest in his view on this question as I am in mine. But Mr. Knox is a monometallist. Mr. Knox believes there ought to be but one coin, and that gold. Now a great many, and very great many men in this country believe that; but I tell you, gentlemen, the time will come—— "

Mr. Knox : "If the gentleman will allow me, I wish to make the statement that I am not a monometallist in the sense which he means. I wish to remain on the gold standard, but nevertheless I am willing to agree to as free a use of silver as possible, while still maintaining that standard. I am willing to increase the coinage of silver from $2,000,000 to $2,500,000 per month. But I want the silver certificates which are based on the silver dollars to always remain so close to the value of the gold dollar that no man, rich or poor, can hereafter lose any thing by their depreciation.

" I want this silver certificate to be always worth 100 cents in gold. I believe in a single gold standard, supplemented by the use of all the silver dollars that can be kept at par in gold. This is not monometallism in the sense used by the gentleman, who would give the impression that I am against the use of any silver whatever.

" I have therefore introduced a resolution providing that hereafter in the issue of silver certificates, such certificates shall be secured by silver bullion worth in the market 100 cents on the dollar. So long as we remain upon the gold standard, so long as the present legal-tender silver-dollar coin remains worth 100 cents, these silver-bullion certificates will be redeemable with the standard-silver dollar. But if we suspend gold payment then the standard-silver dollar will decline in value, and in that event the holder of these silver-bullion certificates shall be entitled to receive the full face value of these certificates in silver bullion at its market value. Use both gold and silver for our currency, but maintain the silver dollar at par with the gold dollar. I want to keep the two metals as close together as possible, so that a man who has debts to pay can pay them in gold value ; and you, gentlemen, who have money loaned out can receive back in payment an equivalent to a dollar in gold. This is my proposition ; these are my views.

" I wish all the bankers of the country to be able to pay their depositors, like honest men, in the same coin which they have received ; or, at least, to return them the value of the money which they received on deposit.

"The issue of silver certificates hereafter based on their bullion value will prevent, without the possibility of doubt, loss to either debtor or creditor.

"I thank the gentleman from Kentucky for giving me the opportunity for expressing my views upon the resolution which I presented to the convention. I intended to have made this explanation at the outset, but these remarks upon the resolution were inadvertently omitted."

It is proper to say that the proposition under consideration was subsequently considered by the Executive Council of the American Banking Association, to whom it was referred, and resulted in a vote of 16 to 3 against the measure. The report of the Council can be obtained upon application to the Association.

The Secretary of the Treasury in his very able and interesting report just issued (December, 1889), proposes to issue certificates based upon the market value of silver. He declined to recommend that these certificates should be a legal tender between individuals, and believed that such an issue would be unconstitutional.

He said : "While our circulation now embraces gold and silver coin and four kinds of paper money, there is in reality, since 1873, but one standard. Section 3,511, Revised Statutes, provides that 'the gold coin of the United States shall be a one dollar piece, which at the standard weight of 25.8 grains shall be the unit of value.' . . . Our legal-tender notes have behind them, in the vaults of the Treasury, a reserve of $100,000,000 in gold provided as a guarantee for their redemption. Our bank currency is based upon United States bonds, the principal and interest of which are payable in gold. Our gold certificates are expressly made redeemable in gold coin."

Kansas City is the first point of interest west of St. Louis, just on the border line between Missouri and Kansas, situated on the Missouri side, but in acknowledgment of the fact that the city is built by, for, and from the products of the "Sunflower State," it was named Kansas City. The growth and prosperity of this city is phenomenal. The immense stores, packing houses, and railroads—steam, cable, elevated, and horse-car lines,—all combined to amaze us beyond expression. It is difficult to convince a New Yorker that there is any thing solid west of the Hudson River. We found substantial prosperity west of the Missouri. Kansas City hotels are not surpassed in this country. Our host had secured for the party elegant rooms and parlors at the Coates House ; but to give us evidence that "The Coates" was not the only first-class hotel in the city, he invited us to breakfast and dine at "The Midland." We were served in the private dining-room. Would any of us decline a breakfast like that served on Wednesday morning, Sept. 25, 1889, at the Midland Hotel ? After two full days of enjoyment and sight-seeing we returned to our house on wheels, and retired to rest, realizing that we should be transported during our sleep to another city and another State—Kansas,—one of the youngest of the sisterhood of States, and also one of the seven surplus-producing agricultural States of the Union.

For the purpose of giving us ample opportunity to witness the growth of Kansas in material wealth and moral power, Mr. Blanchard invited us to make a careful inspection and tour of the State, and see for ourselves if its prosperity and wonderful resources had been fully stated, or even approximately understood, by the bankers and business men of New York.

Friday morning the sun rose bright and clear. It found our car on the side track commanding a magnificent view of one of the finest boulevards of Topeka, the capital of- this great prohibition State. We had hardly finished breakfast when eight elegant carriages dashed up to the car. In a few moments we were being rapidly driven up the boulevard to the Hotel Throop, where we were welcomed by manager Doolittle, a friend of Mr. Blanchard. After being shown to our rooms, we again entered our carriages and were treated to a most enjoyable drive through the principal streets and avenues of this most beautiful city. After calling at the principal banks we returned to our palatial quarters at the Hotel Throop, where we were honored with a call by a special committee from the Board of Trade.

The Hotel Throop is sufficient evidence that prohibition does not damage the business of a first-class hotel. Mrs. James questioned the driver of her carriage, a very bright and intelligent man, and his testimony was positive in favor of prohibition as a benefit to his business.

Hon. D. O. Bradley interviewed the superintendent of police. The testimony from the police department showed a decrease in the number of arrests by the police of the city of Topeka. For the month of September, 1889, they were only one half the number for September, 1882, with double the population in 1889.

Mr. Doolittle had prepared for us a special menu.

The banquet room and tables were most elegantly decorated with beautiful flowers. We were so taken up with the attractions of the table that the hours passed by unheeded. The telephone recalled us to the stern realities of life by announcing that our car was attached to the Westbound " Thunderbolt " and that train of thirteen coaches crowded with through passengers was awaiting our presence in the "Dalmatia." We hurried to our carriages and were driven at full speed to our car, and before we had hardly recovered our breath Topeka had vanished and the broad prairie was in sight.

The whole afternoon was spent in watching the panorama of cities and towns, farms and ranches, creeks and rivers, as we rushed by them. For nearly the whole distance between Topeka and Emporia we passed through one of the great coal-fields of Kansas. After leaving Emporia and the noted limestone quarries of Strong City, our path lay through an almost continuous field of corn, until we reached the thriving city of Newton. After a moment's stop we rushed on through wheat, corn, and oats until the famous Arkansas Valley was reached, and Hutchinson loomed in view. Our car was soon on the *house* track, and we found a large company awaiting to welcome us, among whom were : S. W. Campbell, Esq., President First National Bank ; John Lowry, Esq., President Iowa Town Company ; George S. Bourne, Esq.,

Treasurer Empire Loan and Trust Company; J. R. Pope, Esq., Cashier Valley State Bank; F. R. Chrisman, Esq., Cashier People's State Bank; Samuel Matthews, Esq.; Miles Taylor, Editor *Daily News;* E. L. Meyer, Esq., Cashier First National Bank; W. T. Atkinson, Esq., Cashier National Bank of Commerce; James McKinstry, Esq., Attorney at Law; A. J. Lusk, Esq., President Hutchinson National Bank; W. R. Bennett, Esq., Vice-President Empire Loan and Trust Company, and many others. They crowded our spacious hotel car, and introductions followed. At the request of the party, presented by a committee of ladies, Mr. Knox consented to deliver to us the address which he had prepared for response to the toast, "The East," at the "Bankers' Banquet," of the American Bankers' Association, at Kansas City. Did orator ever have a more unique auditorium or attentive and appreciative audience?

He said: "No American, returning home, can sail through the beautiful harbor and bay of New York without experiencing a thrill of joy and pride at the unequalled location of this great Eastern city and the rapid strides with which it attracts and combines all the elements which have heretofore formed the largest cities of the world! The Germans drink their bumpers, at home and abroad, to the river Rhine. The river Hudson was the first link of communication between the East and the West. Eighty years or more ago our fathers celebrated the opening of the Erie Canal with a joy unequalled by any of our modern celebrations. They felt that the East and the West were brought more closely together by adding this second link to the methods of transportation.

" I remember when a boy to have visited the cabin of one of the passenger packets of the Erie Canal at nightfall. It reminded me of the buttery of my grandmother in the country on the farm, which was a long room with pans of milk placed on shelves on either side, with a narrow passage between. In this cabin, instead of glistening pans of milk, the passengers were laid to sleep upon the shelves. Outside, three horses on the towpath drew the boat, and upon the horses were boys to guide them. Soon after nightfall the boys were asleep, the horses were asleep, and if the boat had been called "Somnambula," every thing would have been in harmony with the name ! The passengers were three weeks making the journey from New York to Chicago by canal and the lakes. If there was a storm upon the lakes there was danger that they might never reach their destination ! Yet our fathers rejoiced over even this small improvement in their means of transportation.

" Within a few months, chiefly by the employment of Eastern as well as Western Capital, perfect lines of railroad have been built and recent improvements have been made, which have so shortened the distance between Chicago and New York that a breakfast can be taken in New York and upon the following day repeated in the city of Chicago. Yet so blasé have we become that this perfect system of transportation has gone into effect almost without public acknowledgment.

" The East and the West then have reason to love the beautiful Hudson, with its Palisades, its Catskill, its West Point, and its

> ' Villages strewn like jewels on a chain
> All its bright length.'

The Mohawk Valley beyond, excels even the Hudson in pastoral beauty.

> ' Whole miles of level grain,
> With leagues of meadow-land and pasture-field,
> Cover its surface ; gray roads wind about,
> O'er which the farmer's wagon clattering rolls,
> And the red mail-coach.   Bridges cross the streams,
> Roofed, with great spider-webs of beams within.
> Homesteads to homesteads flash their window-gleams,
> Like friends that talk by language of the eye.
> Upon its iron strips the engine shoots,
> That half-tamed savage with its boiling heart
> And flaming veins, its warwhoop and its plume.
> Swift as the swallow skims that engine fleets
> Through all the streaming landscape of green field
> And lovely village.   On their pillared lines,
> Distances flash to distances their thoughts,
> And all is one abode of all the joy
> And happiness that civilization yields ! '

" Out from the Mohawk, is Saratoga, and delicious
Lake George, and beyond, the Adirondacks with its
wealth of forest and beauty, its lofty pine trees and its
loftiest mountain peak which we call Mt. Marcy, but
which our Indian Fathers with more aptitude named
'Ta haw us,'—'He splits the sky!' Beyond is the
glorious St. Lawrence with its thousand islands, and
Ontario and Erie which encircle the lands of the
Onondagas, the Cayugas, and the Senecas with their
little sparkling lakes ; and between our own confines
and the border of Her Majesty's Dominions is that
most sublime sentinel of the whole continent—grand
old Niagara !

"The Western man, more frequently than the Eastern,
travels throughout the Commonwealth of Pennsylvania,
and appreciates its soil and climate, its wonderful
resources of coal and iron, and its commercial city of
Philadelphia, with its thousands of pleasant homes and
its hundreds of beautiful industries. Its sister states of
New Jersey and Maryland are on either side and baby
Delaware between. Baltimore is the birthplace of the
song of the 'Star-Spangled Banner.' If there are
those who do not particularly enjoy the scenery of
mountain and forest, brook and river, and bay and
valley of these Commonwealths, there is no one, I am
sure, who does not love the fish and the crabs and the
oysters and the canvas-back duck of the Chesapeake,

which is the most beautiful and bountiful public larder of the universe! And close to Baltimore is magnificent Washington, the capital of our common country. In another direction to the east is Bunker Hill and Boston Harbor and the ' Hub,' and all the people ' way down East' who have for eighty years been sending their sons to the West to found great commonwealths like Kentucky and Ohio, Indiana and Illinois, Minnesota and Kansas, and other wonderful States like those that surround us, and others still upon the more and more distant frontier.

" The children of the East are proud of the East and the children of the West are proud of the West. I lived for a number of years in Minnesota when it was a territory, and I am told by my friends that I made the Eastern people—to use a slang expression—' tired ' in singing the praises of the land of the Dakotas. After I had located myself in New York, upon a return from a visit to Minnesota I met an old friend in Chicago with whom I had an earnest conversation in reference to the rapid progress of the West. We were both Western men in our enthusiasm, but when he found that I had located in New York he expressed his dissatisfaction by saying : ' New York ! Why, in a few years New York will be to Chicago what Liverpool is to London ; New York, like Liverpool, will be the seaport town, but Chicago, like London, will be the great interior city ! ' His sudden exclamation nearly took me from my feet, but when I recovered I answered him as earnestly : ' When Chicago reaches its population of fifteen hundred thousand New York will add to its boundaries a few of its suburbs like Brooklyn and Jersey City and Newark and Hoboken, when it will have a population of three millions, and give Chicago another pull of half a century ! '

'' But I have been in the habit for years of visiting the West frequently, in order to watch its progress and study geography,—for seeing is believing. I have just spent two days in Chicago, and now find myself for the first time in Kansas City, which was called by more than one person in Chicago whom I met, ' Chicago No. 2 ! ' And I have come to the conclusion that possibly what my enthusiastic Chicago friend said, and what I heard Governor Seward also say in the city of St. Paul in the year 1856, is true—' that somewhere here, in the State of Illinois, the State of Kansas, or the State of Minnesota— somewhere here in this galaxy of States, which we call the Northwest, there will be built a great interior city, larger than any of our seaport towns.'

'' The Eastern cities will however, for years contest with you the right to excel them in population, in intelligence, and in wealth. We acknowledge your rapid progress. We know that forty years ago Chicago had just begun to exist and that many of your other cities were unknown.

" But while you have been growing the East has grown rapidly. Take, for instance, the increase in bank corporations and banking capital, as an example. The capital and surplus of the banks of the East during the last thirty years have greatly increased. The increase in their deposits in the last twenty years has been without parallel in any other country. There has been an enormous increase in the deposits of savings-banks, which are properly institutions conducted not for the benefit of the shareholders, but solely for the benefit of the depositors. The deposits of the New England States in savings-banks were but 43 millions of dollars in 1852 ; in 1860, but 148 millions ; they are now more than 1,190 millions. The deposits of the savings-banks of the State of New York in 1852 were less than 28 millions ; they are now 505 millions. The capital of the banks of New York City during the last thirty years has increased from 35 millions to 80 millions, and a surplus of 40 millions has been accumulated. The loans have increased many times, and the individual deposits more than seven times, while the bank balances have increased in much greater ratio. Thirty years ago there was no clearing-house. In the year 1854 the exchanges were 5,000 millions ; they are now 31,000 millions. The daily exchanges were 19 millions ; they are now 101 millions. In the month of October of last year, according to the comptroller's report, there was

an increase of 469 millions over the previous year in
the exchanges at the clearing-houses of the United
States, of which increase 215 millions was in New
York, 84 millions in Boston, 35 millions in Philadelphia, and 56 millions in Chicago. From a slip cut
from the Chicago *Tribune* on my way to this city, I
find that the gross exchanges of the clearing-houses of
the United States on September 21, 1889, was 1,044
millions, of which 663 millions was in the city of New
York and 381 millions outside of New York. This slip
contains returns from the clearing-houses of fifty different cities, including all the larger cities. The clearings
of the city of Boston were $82,000,000, of Philadelphia
$74,000,000, of Chicago $69,000,000, of St. Louis $20,-
000,000, and of Kansas City $9,000,000.

" In the year 1861 I compiled a table showing at a
glance the total receipts of the national banks on two
different days, and the proportion of these receipts by
the banks in the various cities. These returns show
that while the total receipts upon a certain day were
$295,000,000, the receipts of forty-eight banks in the
city of New York were $165,000,000, or nearly 56 per
cent. of the whole. The receipts of the four great cities
of New York, Philadelphia, Boston, and Chicago, com-
prised nearly four fifths of the total receipts on June 30,
1881, and nearly three fourths of the total on September
17, 1881 ; while the sixteen reserved cities on June 30th

were more than 85 per cent., and on September 17th more than 82 per cent., of the whole amount.

"These facts show how closely connected is the business of the banks elsewhere with the great commercial cities of the East. Nearly every bank and banker located in all the principal cities and villages of the country have deposits subject to sight draft in New York. Every mail not only brings remittances from neighboring cities, but from the most inaccessible points in the country. To-day a single roadside tavern or outpost upon the great plains of the frontier; to-morrow a railroad is constructed, and in place of the tavern of the frontiersman or the military outpost, there is the city of Cheyenne in the embryo State of Wyoming, or the city of Bismarck in the new State of Dakota, or the city of Winnipeg in the Provinces of Manitoba. And almost on the day of the birth of these young cities or villages, banks are organized under the authority of the laws of the United States or Canada, which are almost immediately thereafter brought into close communication with some correspondent in New York.

"The East sympathizes with you in your growth, and receives substantial profit from that source. New York, as well as Chicago, is your market, and the effect of good crops in all sections of the West is felt in New York as surely as in your Western cities. The progress and prosperity of the West increases largely the progress and prosperity of the East. For more than a half century—for more than eighty years—the East has been sending a portion of its surplus here for investment. It had its early losses, but its gains have been large, which is evident from the fact that it has never for a single year ceased to send, not only its people here, to find homes in the new States, but it has increased its Western investments annually. A few years ago tables were made showing the distribution of national-bank stock throughout the country, from which it was found that a large portion—say about one eighth—of the stock of these new institutions in the West was held in the East. If it were possible it would be most interesting to obtain similar figures in reference to the holdings of the East in your railroad and other transportation companies, and in your industries of various kinds. It is known that the East in many instances holds a majority of the stock in your greatest companies, and annually elects the officers of such corporations. The interest upon the bonds, almost without exception, of all your Western corporations, is payable in New York, and to considerable extent to Eastern owners. You have grown rich ; but we of the East are your co-partners in business, and notwithstanding your riches, we give notice that we do not intend there shall be any DISSOLUTION OF THE CO-PARTNERSHIP.

"So far from that being the case, we give notice that in those branches of business which we find most profitable, we intend from year to year to increase our holdings. Those of us who have been in the habit of visiting the growing West, know its resources, and propose, as heretofore, to continue to assist in its development—largely under your management.

"We do not care to prophesy where the centre of this great country will be a century hence. The important point is, that the country, as a whole, shall increase its power, its population, its wealth; that its people shall be intelligent and homogeneous in character; and, above all, that the country shall have a government that is good and strong. I lived in Minnesota when St. Paul had a population of about 5,000. At our social gatherings we frequently took a census, and always found that every State in the East was represented by persons present. The East is the father, and grandfather, and great-grandfather of the West. The telegraph, the railroad, the telephone, and the cable have made us all neighbors!

"Webster, in one of his great speeches, said of South Carolina and Massachusetts: 'Shoulder to shoulder they went through the Revolution; hand in hand they stood around the Administration of Washington, and felt his strong arm lean upon them for support.' We may paraphrase this expression, and say that with the rapid development of each section of the country, it is most important that the East and the West, the North and the South, shall, if necessary, march shoulder to shoulder in defence of the country, hand in hand stand around every good Administration in time of trouble, and rejoice if the strong arm of the Executive shall lean upon all for support ! "

After we had enjoyed this treat and all expressed our appreciation of it, we looked out upon the beauties of a Kansas moonlight night. The charm was too much for us. In a moment we were upon the street.

Electric light was everywhere, making night almost as bright as day. The long line of beautifully decorated show windows of the large stores reminded us of home.

Mr. Blanchard had secured elegant rooms for our party at the Brunswick, but most of us preferred our cosy apartments on the " Dalmatia."

We were all up bright and early, after a good night's sleep. This Kansas atmosphere is wonderful. It makes one sleep at night in spite of himself, and such an appetite as it does give.

As we came from the breakfast table we found elegant carriages awaiting us.

Each bank sent out either its President or Cashier to help entertain us.

We visited the wonderful salt works at South Hutchinson. The pure white salt was admired by all. Being

RIVERSIDE SALT WORKS, HUTCHINSON, KANSAS.

free from all impurities, the Hutchinson salt does not cake. The supply is unlimited ; at a depth of 350 to 400 feet lies a bed of solid, pure rock-salt, 330 feet thick, covering an area of many miles in extent. Hutchinson will supply all the salt trade west of the Mississippi River. Additional interest was manifested by all in this field, as it was learned that this source of wealth was originally developed by Ben Blanchard, unaided and alone.

The development of the great salt wealth of South Hutchinson no doubt gave Hutchinson permanent impulse at the opportune moment. Competition from Wichita for the business centre that must of necessity settle on some point in Kansas subsided when the salt fields came to the surface with its unlimited supply of pure white salt. Standing by the side of one of the leading bank presidents of Hutchinson, at one of the great salt wells, one of our party, not knowing whose energy and enterprise discovered and developed the great industry, made the remark : '' I should be willing to take off my hat to the man who first struck salt here.'' The bank President replied : '' Well, you may take off your hat to Mr. Blanchard, the President of the Empire Loan and Trust Company.''

We left the salt works, with its thousands of tons of snowy salt, for the green fields of the farms. There was not a cloud in the sky. The cool, fresh, country air put us all in the best of spirits. For miles and miles we hurried on, scaring up quail, prairie chicken, and rabbits from the finely-kept green hedge fences which line the road on both sides. Choice farms are on every hand. In fact the country presents the appearance of a checker-board, nearly every quarter section being a fine farm with its grove of forest trees, orchard, and small fruit. The two story farm-houses and large barns remind one of the best portions of Pennsylvania.

We passed team after team on its way to Hutchinson loaded with wheat, oats, or corn. We stopped at the fine fruit farm of Mr. Switzer, and received a bountiful supply of choice, rosy apples. The cherry and peach trees still bore traces of the wonderful crops that had been gathered and shipped. To our left was Mr. Furney's fine mansion, and a little farther on the elegant stock farm with its hundreds of blooded cattle, belonging to Mr. Stewart. Both of these gentlemen were formerly of Philadelphia. Many other similar places would have been in sight, but the great fields of corn on every hand hid them from our view. The new wheat, which has been sown in abundance, was just coming through the ground, and gave a fresh, green look to many a field.

We reached Hutchinson in time for dinner, and could hardly realize that we had driven over twenty miles.

After a sumptuous dinner at the Brunswick, we visited the chief points of interest in Hutchinson; with the mayor and leading bankers of the city. We were driven past its twelve salt works to the packing-houses of Fowler & Underwood, and Tobey & Booth, and the great lard refinery of Fairbanks & Co., the ice factory, the banks, the home office of the Empire Loan and Trust Company, and to the office of the Hutchinson *Daily News* (Ralph L. Easley, Esq., President and managing editor), then to the Santa Fe Hotel, where a banquet had been spread for us by the members of the Hutchinson Clearing-House, who were accompanied by their ladies.

This hospitality was an entire surprise to us. Hon. Darwin R. James, Hon. John Jay Knox, and the Hon. D. O. Bradley expressed our thanks to the citizens of Hutchinson for the courtesies and hospitality extended to us. We take the following from the Hutchinson *News :*

"Before leaving the dining-room the *News* reporter took occasion to inquire of several of the gentlemen how they were impressed with Hutchinson.

" Edward Merritt, Esq., President of Long Island Loan and Trust Company said : ' We have been delighted and surprised at the wonderful development of the State of Kansas. The growth and progress of Hutchinson are marvellous. The discovery by Mr.

Blanchard of the salt fields underlying this section of the country must certainly add largely to the wealth of the city and its inhabitants. The natural advantages of its situation together with the inevitable growth of its industries make the future of Hutchinson, in my judgment, sure beyond doubt.'

"Hon. John J. Knox, who was Comptroller of Currency at Washington for eleven years, said: 'Yes, Hutchinson is indeed a beautiful and also a wonderful town. The geographical position of Hutchinson respecting the great through lines east and west is such, that she is sure to continue to be one of the leading cities in Kansas.'

"Mr. D. Ogden Bradley, President of the Tarrytown National Bank of Tarrytown, N. Y., a member of the Legislature of the State of New York for several years, and a banker of forty years' experience, said: 'I am greatly pleased with Hutchinson, and see elements of great strength and certain prosperity all around it. I greatly admire Kansas. It is rapidly advancing to the lead of the moral and intellectual forces of the nation. It is doing a great work, and has a gigantic future. Hutchinson will certainly become its metropolis.'

"Hon. Darwin R. James, who served in the Forty-eighth and Forty-ninth Congresses, is an importer of indigo and spices, president of a savings-bank, and secretary of the New York Board of Trade and Transportation, said : ' Words fail to express the pleasure of the excursion we are making. Kansas is a magnificent State, and is developing with wonderful rapidity. I thought I knew something about it before I came, but I am amazed at the progress made since my former visit. All that I had heard of Hutchinson, and it was much, has been more than realized. She is a magnificent young city, whose possibilities for the future are unlimited. We might say of Hutchinson " She is the salt of the earth." '

" Dr. Frank W. Shaw, of Brooklyn, N. Y., being asked for his impressions replied that, while not a banker himself, he could appreciate the interest which men of affairs always feel toward the prosperity of any growing section of the West. The opinions of Kansas which he had heard from the distinguished gentlemen with whom he had the pleasure of travelling had shown him the broader views of observation, but what he had personally seen to-day of Hutchinson and its wonderful industries and possibilities convinced him of the soundness of Western enthusiasm. Those magnificent salt works alone assure the future success of the city. He said he should always feel indebted to Mr. Blanchard for his first view of the substantial prosperity of Kansas and of this beautiful city.

"Crowell Hadden, Esq., President of the Long Island Bank of Brooklyn, the oldest bank in the city, said: 'I am highly gratified at the growth and enter-prise of the city. It bids fair to become one of the greatest of Western cities. The recent discovery of salt underlying the city by Mr. Ben Blanchard will add largely to its wealth.'

"Capt. Ambrose Snow, President of the Board of Trade of New York City, said: 'Yes, sir, Hutchin-son has a great future before her. That wonderful salt! Why, it is a revelation to me. With that, and the railroads you have and those you are getting, no power in the world' could prevent Hutchinson from forging right to the front and staying there!'

"The ladies of Mr. Blanchard's party were of much more than ordinary intelligence, and had travelled not a little, and seen much of the world, and were familiar with European scenery. They were charmed with our beautiful streets and neat and handsome business blocks, and elegant lawns and residences. They were unanimous in the opinion that if they could not live in New York they would certainly choose Hutchinson."

Of one fact all were convinced—that Hutchinson could furnish as good social life as we could desire. " Hutchinson's salt mines are valuable, but her women are far above rubies," said a gentleman of our party, and we all said "Amen!"

Our party were delighted and surprised to find in this beautiful city of seventeen thousand people such a rush of business. The streets were thronged with teams, the stores crowded with people. Hundreds of new buildings were going up—great stone blocks and elegant residences. We could easily understand this, when we found that Hutchinson was located on three trunk lines and two branch railroads, surrounded by an agricultural country that cannot be excelled, and underlaid with the thickest vein of pure salt in the world. Mr. Bourne, Treasurer of the Empire Loan and Trust Company, and for many years a banker, told me that a great many of the business men of Hutchinson were formerly from New York, and that Eastern capital was rapidly coming in to develop the latent interests here.

As an illustration of the rapidly growing commercial importance of Hutchinson, the Santa Fé Railroad Co. has recently issued circulars to shippers of live stock, which places Hutchinson on an equal footing with Kansas City.

William Willard Howard, in *Harper's Weekly*, Nov. 3, 1888, says : '' Wise and conservative methods of doing business attract a great deal of New York, Philadelphia, and Boston capital to Kansas properties that are now lying idle. Many Eastern capitalists are sending money to Kansas, but with few exceptions the bulk of the investments are in mortgages on farm property. To men who have made a study of Western securities these mortgages are looked upon as safe and profitable investments; but while they are no doubt beneficial to the individual borrower and lender, they yet cannot benefit Kansas a hundredth part as much as the same money would if used in the proper development of the State's great resources. The day is rapidly approaching when the vast sums of money now stored in financial centres will be as readily invested in Kansas property as funds are at present put into farm mortgages. The city of Hutchinson has shown how it can be done.''

After the banquet we entered our car bound for Colorado; after a short stop at Pueblo we arrived in Denver, and went to the "Windsor," where Mr. Blanchard had secured rooms for all during our stay in this far-off city. So easy and pleasant had been our journey of over 2,000 miles, we could not realize the distance we had travelled, except by the difference of time—we were two hours behind New York time. On Sunday attended service at Trinity M. E. Church, a beautiful building, organ, etc., valued at $300,000. Monday morning, in seven carriages, a representative of the "Bankers' Association of Denver" in each carriage, visited the "Omaha and Grant Smelting Works," public buildings, etc., under the courteous direction of ex-Gov. J. B. Grant. Leaving Denver Monday, 4:45 P.M., the next stop was at Colorado Springs, where there are no springs. We were anxious to reach Manitou, where the springs are numerous. The regular train had left. The necessity for prompt action was apparent. There would be no out train till morning. Mr. Blanchard was equal to the emergency ; a special engine was secured, and with the superintendent of the road as conductor we started on the up grade, and arrived at Manitou (which is the Indian for Great Spirit) safely at eight o'clock of a beautiful evening. Carriages had been ordered, and were waiting at the depot, and a ride through Manitou, up Ruxton Glen to the springs by moonlight, completed the delightful experience of the day.

The " Iron Spring " and " Soda Spring " are superior for health to the "Washington " and "Congress " springs of Saratoga.

UP PIKE'S PEAK, Tuesday, October 1st.

The day was perfect ; not a cloud. Our car stood on the side track of the Midland, at an elevation of seven thousand feet, equal to the " Tip-Top House " on Mt. Washington. All were eager to know if the weather was propitious. Hasty toilets enabled us, one and all, to assemble at an early hour and watch for the first rays of the rising sun. We were looking east, when one of the group, a lady, was the first to call out : " There it is " ; and, turning to the west, we saw " The Peak," snow-clad, blushing like a rose. Then

" Gog and Magog " caught the rays ; then " Cameron's
Cone." The foot-hills followed, one after another, till
all had joined the " Peak " in proclaiming " The sun
has risen." We were charmed by the wonderful and
novel scene. " Manitou " lay asleep at our feet. We
watched till at last we too were standing in the sun-
shine.

After an early breakfast our Pullman Hotel, the
" Dalmatia," was taken over the Midland Railroad
to Cascade City, passing through eight tunnels in
going six miles to ascend about one thousand feet.
We left our Pullman at Cascade City, and took carriages with four horses, for a seventeen-mile climb to
reach the summit. The carriage road is a marvel of
engineering skill. At the half-way house our horses
were changed for four sure-footed mules. After leaving
the timber line the prospect is wonderful, changing
with every turn of the road, and there are eighty turns.

The ascent of Pike's Peak in time of flowers is a surprise for those who expect to see only the rough boulder
and riven rock. " Flowers deck their inclined sides
in great blocks of color, and litter their terraces and
woodland edges in variegated confusion. There is no
difficult pass where they are not found ; no dusky glen
that does not harbor them ; scarcely any height on
which their beauty will not appear to gladden him who
toils to reach the summits."

" 'T is legend told of primal days
  When ' Manitou,' like clay,
The gray rock mountain shapes did raise
  To celebrate his sway.
He was not pleased. The mountains bare
  Were bleak and dull and gray.
He snatched a rainbow from the air,
  To use its colors gay.
Crumbling its bars, with chanted spell,
  Their radiant dust he threw,
And everywhere a handful fell
  A million flow'rets grew."

As the early snow on the mountains had killed the flowers before our visit, a volume of pressed " Wild Flowers from the Rockies " was presented to each one of our party by our host. The flowers were gone but the Autumn tints had painted the grand old mountain, emerald, garnet, and gold.

Miss L. I. S. says :

" One curious fact I remember was, that the pine trees all presented branches on but one side of the trunk, and that the south, for the bleak north winds prove too severe for growth on that side, and instead of growing up, like well regulated trees, the branches all hang down, bended by their weight of snow, presenting a very singular appearance.

" How many times our blood would run cold as we

skirted a particularly sharp turn on the edge of a very steep precipice.

"Snow was very plenty about us, and often we would be driving through piles two and three feet deep in some sheltered portion of the road.

" Imagine, ye who were not there, sinking in above the hubs in snow, genuine snow in its pristine beauty, and then you can realize why his lordship, the Peak, looks so white at a distance. And now comes the time for the furs and mittens and lap-robes, and were it not for the bright sun I imagine some noses would have been very blue.

"We had an unusually clear day for our visit, just what our favored party might have expected, for what was there that did not present its most attractive side to us.

" Before we quite reach the summit we get a grand view of the Continental Divide and Snowy Range, and those two white icebergs to the south they tell us are the Spanish Peaks, one hundred and eighty miles away.

" And now we have almost finished our seventeen miles of climbing, and the high mountains that we have come over lie like level plains beneath us, and nothing obstructs our view ; we are head and shoulders above the world. Up, up, until the Tip-Top House comes in sight, and we draw up before it and alight cautiously, so as to take the rarefied air by degrees into our lungs. ◄

" The Peak was reached at one o'clock. The sun was shining with mid-day brightness. The moon was also shining, undimmed by the sun's brighter rays. To the east, " Manitou " and " Colorado Springs " seemed floating in space ; to the north and west, Gray's Peak, and the Snowy Range, and the smoke of the smelters at Leadville, seventy-five miles away ; to the south, the " Spanish Peaks," snow-clad, one hundred and eighty miles off, seemed only a few miles across the mountains. We stood fourteen thousand three hundred and thirty-six feet above New York and Brooklyn.

" At about 2.30 o'clock we stow ourselves in the stages and begin our trip down the mountain, a much easier but more thrilling ride. Mrs. Hadden, I think, voiced the experience of some of the rest when she said she only took two breaths all the way down—one when she started, and another when she stopped. It *was* exciting to be whirled around the sharp curves, at a rapid gait, especially when an overturned cart told the tale of some poor fellow coming to grief; but it really amused us to picture the antics the little donkey must have gone through in his involuntary tobogganing down the side of the mountain. Several of the turns were marvellous, the road almost returning on itself, and in one spot we could see seven different portions of the road in its serpentine windings.

" Shall this pleasure ever end ?   Must we come down
to every one's level ?

" The sun has just disappeared behind the snow-clad
peak.   We can still see it shining on Cameron's Cone
and on the peaks to our left.

> ' The western waves of ebbing day
>   Rolled o'er the glen their level way ;
>   Each purple peak, each flinty spire,
>   Was bathed in floods of living fire.
>   But not a setting beam could glow
>   Within the dark ravines below,
>   Where twined the path in shadow hid,
>   Round many a rocky pyramid,
>   Shooting abruptly from the dell
>   Its thunder-splintered pinnacle ;
>   Round many an insulated mass,
>   The native bulwarks of the pass,
>   Huge as the towers which builders vain
>   Presumptuous piled on Shinar's plain,
>   Their rocky summits, split and rent,
>   Formed turret, dome, or battlement,
>   Or seemed fantastically set
>   With cupola or minaret,
>   Wild crests as pagod ever decked,
>   Or mosque of Eastern architect.'

" At six o'clock we whirl into Cascade.   We jump
from the stages, and fairly pinch ourselves to see if we
are the same people who left there in the morning.

Yes, we are the same in outward appearance, but something has entered into our lives, our inner selves, that broadens us out, and will prove a continual feast in coming days.

" It would seem that a climax could hardly be capped, but ours was in a most delightful way. The stages had hardly driven away when up drive four or five carriages, and we are invited to go back to Manitou, by way of the Ute Pass trail, instead of by the railroad. Nothing loath we get in, and settle ourselves for one of the pleasantest of rides. It is a perfect evening, and we have not gone far before the moon comes out and throws a spell of enchantment over the scene. The road is so smooth and hard that our horses' hoofs make a pleasant ring as we speed along. A merry little stream, whose dashing and dancing have given it the name of " The Fountain that Boils," accompanies us, and we run a race with it, but own ourselves thoroughly beaten in all respects, when our rival enhances its beauty, redoubles its speed, and makes louder its laughter as it throws itself headlong down the cliff of rocks ; and we alight from our carriage to go down the ravine and pay homage to the beauties of Rainbow Falls.

" This brief glimpse in the twilight makes us long for a view by day, and we promise ourselves a longer visit the next time we come."

As we bowl along we look up at the steep, rocky walls of the cañon, shutting us in from all disturbing thoughts and sights, and the moon floods all with its peaceful light, and all fatigue and disquiet vanishes, and we realize that we are having a fitting ending to a glorious day.

The electric lights at Manitou recall us to ourselves, and we finish a well-rounded day, begun with Pike's Peak by sunrise, and we leave him sleeping under the watchful eye of the purest moon that ever shone.

Wednesday, October 2d.

Another brilliant day. An early breakfast. Carriages were taken for the most wonderful drive of the trip. First to " Iron Springs " and " Ruxton Glen," then to the "Garden of the Gods," more wonderful than can be told ; then to " Glen Eyrie " ; then the " Messa Road "—who will forget the beauty of its scenery ?

We then turned our way to the scene of what was to be the culmination of our journey. As we approached Cheyenne Mountain, memories of (H. H.) Helen Hunt Jackson, arose in every mind. Her solitary grave upon Cheyenne Mountain, selected by herself, is unmarked, except as friendship's hand has raised a mound of small stones and pieces of marble, an evidence of affection more significant than formal monument could be. It is an illustration of one of her own verses :

GATEWAY, GARDEN OF THE GODS.

.

" But no decaying
Can reach it in this sepulchre, whose stone
Our hearts must make !   To an exceeding glory grown,
This grief outweighing."

In Cheyenne Cañon where, almost imprisoned by the perpendicular rocks, lunch was eaten with keen relish, and the health of our host drank with cool, foaming "Manitou Spring water," Wall Street was forgotten. Attention was directed to a prominent Wall Street bank president sitting on a rock enjoying the bountiful collation, with two young ladies acting as waitresses.

After lunch we rambled through the beautiful cañon and visited the Falls, where for 500 feet cascade follows cascade, till in "Seven Falls" they reach the bottom of the cañon.

How reluctantly we entered our carriages, for it was to be our last drive on this delightful journey.   The "Pillars of Hercules" from a height of 1,500 feet looked down upon us with approval, and the "Seven Falls" united with us in singing the "Doxology." We drove back to Colorado Springs and through its principal streets to our inviting quarters in the "Dalmatia," ever ready to welcome us.

The next morning we were again riding through the fertile fields of Kansas.   A brief stop at Hutchinson to say good-bye to Messrs. Burns and Bennett, thence to Topeka, Kansas City, St. Louis, and home, via the Big

Four System to Indianapolis and Cleveland, thence by Lake Shore and New York Central, reaching Grand Central Depot on time Saturday evening, October 5th.

Probably no one enjoyed the trip more than Edward Merritt, Esq., President of the Long Island Loan and Trust Company. We had not finished the first day's travel when, on account of a striking resemblance, Mr. Merritt was recognized by the crowd at the depot as President Harrison. This gave him a *prestige* and popularity with the party that continued. Should any of us need counsel, we appealed to him. The young ladies always did. Did they fall, Mr. Merritt was expected to help them up. Captain Snow, when accused of sleeping soundly, was delighted to secure his counsel, and from his judgment there was no appeal.

One of the advantages of such a trip is safety. To travel over 4,000 miles involves some risks apparent to all. To have a skilful physician and surgeon at hand in Dr. Frank W. Shaw was duly appreciated. We had not gone 1,000 miles before a spark intruded the sacred precincts of one of the brightest eyes that ever looked upon the wonders of the " Garden of the Gods." The cry for Dr. Shaw was promptly answered by skilful relief. How often that cry was made and responded to the Doctor's " Diary " will attest. The youngest and oldest alike shared his skill and watchful care.

At Topeka J. R. Mulvane, Esq., President of the Bank of Topeka, gave me the following statement :

The corn crop this year will be about two hundred and fifty million bushels. (The Secretary of Kansas State Board of Agriculture raises this estimate to 276,541,338 bushels.) The wheat crop forty million bushels ; oats fifty million bushels ; rye and barley ten million bushels ; flax-seed five million bushels ; pork, in 1873, the State supplied 67,500 hogs ; in 1889, one million eight hundred and seventy thousand (1,870,000).

Mr. Mulvane says, the products of Kansas farms *this year alone*, if applied, would liquidate every dollar of indebtedness. The following lines by Mrs. Sigourney may be very appropriately applied to Kansas ·

" The sturdy reapers sing, garnering the corn
 That feedeth other realms besides their own.
 Toil lifts his brawny arm, and takes the wealth
 That makes his children princes ;
 Strange steeds of iron, with their ceaseless freight,
 Tramp night and day ; while the red lightning bears
 Thy slightest whisper on its wondrous wing."

While in Denver, Colorado, we visited the Smelting Works, the great industry of that solid and thriving city. Ore is brought direct from some of the larger mines of the State and extensive shipments of ore and copper "matte" are received from Montana, Utah, New Mexico, and other western territories.

The value of the shipments from one of the many smelters this year will be from $3,500,000 to $4,000,000. This is a small fraction of the wealth developed in hard cash by one of the youngest cities of the West. This goes to New York banks to increase their capital and swell their surplus. If all the bank presidents of New York would follow Mr. Knox's example and visit and personally inspect the solid growth and security the West offers for investments, they would all say with him : "You have grown rich, but we of the East are your co-partners in business, and notwithstanding your riches, we give notice that we do not intend there shall be any dissolution of the co-partnership. So far from that being the case, we give notice that in those branches of business which we find most profitable, we intend from year to year to increase our holdings. Those of us who have been in the habit of visiting the growing West, know its resources and propose, as heretofore, to continue to assist in the development—largely under your management."

After leaving Albany it was evident that our pleasure-trip would soon terminate and we should be obliged to say "good-bye." As usual, and without formality, Mr. James was asked to call to order and take the chair. His address was expressive of the feelings of the whole party when he said that one and all wished to express to Mr. Ben Blanchard their sincere appreciation of his cordial courtesy and unlimited hospitality during a two weeks' trip, upon which every anticipation had been more than realized, and that he was well aware that while we had all been so well cared for, without an anxious thought, the trip had cost Mr. Blanchard severe care and attention. Mr. Knox followed, and said that the two weeks' vacation had been the most delightful trip he had ever taken. Mr. Merritt joined in acknowledging the enjoyment that had been complete. Mr. Bradley, Captain Snow, Dr. Shaw, and Mr. Hadden all gave expression to the same feelings of appreciation and gratification. The last and best speech came impromptu from the youngest member of the company.

Mr. Blanchard was very evidently pleased with the kind words of appreciation for his hospitality that had been spoken. He said in response :

" My friends, you give me too much credit. I am glad to admit that we have had a happy time ; but I could not have made the trip a success without the aid of all of your good offices.

" The railroad officials have contributed their courtesies without stint. The Pullman Company have shown us every attention.

" We have been favored with perfect weather, and saved from accident.

"You have each one joined in making every hour full of brightness, good cheer, and happiness. You have made me indebted to you for the pleasure you have given me. You have honored me with your presence, and I shall ever cherish your kind words, looks, and actions."

Mr. Blanchard's reply was a surprise to all. We had all given expression to the feeling that the two weeks just closing were the most enjoyable we had ever experienced in our journeyings ; but no thought had entered our minds that this was the most delightful trip our host had ever enjoyed, for we knew he had taken a dozen similar pleasure-parties to the Yellowstone, California, Minnesota, and other points of interest. To hear him say that our company had placed him under obligations, was truly capping the climax.

The pleasure of all our company was increased by the presence of Mrs. Blanchard, who returned to New York with us. When mention is made of our host, we always include Mrs. Blanchard.

After our return home, the party selected a beautiful present of sterling silverware, inscribed as follows :

To Mrs. BEN BLANCHARD,
from the Dalmatia Party, Sept. 23, 1889.

The New York *World* of October 7th contained the following :

" A party of New Yorkers, who have been travelling in the West for ten days in a special car, the guests of Ben Blanchard, Esq., arrived home late Saturday evening. The party numbered about twenty. Mr. Knox, who was for many years Comptroller of the Currency at Washington, went on ahead of the party to attend a meeting of the National Banking Association in Kansas City, and joined them there. It was thought that their trip might have some connection with some new financial scheme to be developed in the West, but Mr. Knox said yesterday that they had gone simply for pleasure. All declared that they had a most delightful time.

" ' The West is developing rapidly,' said Mr. Knox. ' It would pay every Eastern business to make a journey through the West every two or three years.' ''

Was ever pleasure and profit so delightfully combined ? After leaving the Bankers' Convention at Kansas City all care or thought of business was dismissed. We were in the watch-care of Mr. Blanchard, and, confident that he knew the way, we all surrendered ourselves to his protection. My second visit was just three months after my first. Then the crops were waving in the fields, now they were harvested ; and as the Hon. Darwin R. James said in his address at the banquet at Hutchinson, " All that Major Corwin has told us about the crops and the salt and the condition of things in Kansas has been more than realized.''

The '' Dalmatia Party '' is now scattered. Two are in Europe. Others are again controlling the finances of Wall Street, and the busy marts of trade and commerce of the East, while our host is engaged as before in developing the undiscovered wealth of the great agricultural State, which has untold riches of salt and other interests besides,—Kansas. May he go on from conquering to conquest, from success to success, is the wish of all those who enjoyed his unselfish hospitality.

GOOD-BY '' DALMATIA.''

Our house on wheels, in which we travelled safely over 4,000 miles, was about seventy feet long, by ten feet wide ; one story ; divided into drawing-room, smoking-room, kitchen, and large family room. For two weeks we enjoyed its close quarters,—small for the residence of twenty-two people. But it was the people that made the rooms delightful.

> '' Some love the glow of outward show,
>   Some love mere wealth and try to win it ;
>   The house to me may lowly be,
>   If I but like the people in it.
>   What 's all the gold that glitters cold,
>   When linked to hard or haughty feeling ?

Whate'er we 're told, the nobler gold
Is truth of heart and manly dealing !
Then let them seek, whose minds are weak,
Mere fashion's smile, and try to win it ;
The house to me may lowly be,
If I but like the people in it ! "

THE END.

www.ingramcontent.com/pod-product-compliance
Lightning Source LLC
Chambersburg PA
CBHW021515090426
42739CB00007B/626